D0616994

la⌣gh

Everyday laughter healing
for greater happiness
and wellbeing

lisa sturge

quadrille

CONTENTS

foreword

Laughter is a language that everyone understands. Sharing laughter with others brings a deep sense of connection and belonging, immersing us in the present moment. Laughter enables us to communicate joyfully, to release stress and to experience deep relaxation.

In this book we are encouraged to find inventive ways of bringing laughter into our lives as a deliberate choice; instead of waiting for laughter to arrive, actively choose to laugh! When we decide to bring laughter to the body, regardless of mood or circumstance, we free ourselves from the limitations of our conditioned and habitual responses.

The health benefits of laughter outlined in this book are widespread, with news stories flooding in every day that verify the extraordinary and powerful effects of laughter on the mind, body and spirit.

I encourage all my students around the world to keep spreading laughter far and wide. Hopefully one day we will see lasting peace in the world through greater awareness, shared love, unconditional laughter and deeper understanding.

Whether you have been laughing for a while or have not laughed in a very long time, this little book provides a treasure trove of creative suggestions to help you along the laughter path. I wish you all well for the laughter journey that awaits and may you discover unexpected joy and inner peace along the way.

Dr. Madan Kataria
Founder of the Worldwide Laughter Yoga Movement

DO YOU REMEMBER THE LAST TIME YOU REALLY LAUGHED?

It may have been...

during a trolley race around the supermarket on a routine weekly shop...

when you walked into the kitchen and found your partner grooving to the radio in just an apron...

while playing a game of 'Tag' with your Yorkshire terrier...

when you glimpsed yourself in the mirror to find an albatross had made a nest in your hair...

when you and your sibling decided to decorate your faces with chocolate warrior paint while baking...

while singing and dancing with abandon in the office corridor just as your boss walked through the door...

watching your favourite comedian in a live stand-up show...

in-between loud screams on the scariest roller coaster ever...

during a laughter club session where you ended up rolling around on the floor with others in fits of giggles...

when you and your friend suddenly laughed for no apparent reason at all and then found yourselves unable to stop...

THERE ARE A MULTITUDE OF REASONS WHY WE LAUGH.

Laughter can surprise us, coming from nowhere, throwing us into convulsions of mirth. During the most serious of events we can become overwhelmed with a burning desire to laugh wildly, clutching our heaving sides till they ache and hanging on to respectability by our fingernails.

So where did laughter come from and how did it evolve?

Laughter is a bridge between people. It enables us to express joy and playfulness and to share our delight with others. Laughter encourages us to be more of who we are, rather than who we think we should be. It is an ancient, free tool that has been around for millions of years; laughter is an instant equaliser, a shock absorber and a community builder.

The multiple benefits of laughter can have a wide ranging impact; strengthening our relationships, improving our health and increasing our efficiency in the workplace. Laughter brings relaxation and refreshment to everyday activities; it frees us from our habitual patterns and makes us glow from the inside out. Laughter reminds us to stop and smell the roses, then to laugh when a greenfly crawls up our nostril.

Even if we have not laughed for a really long time, laughter is a skill that can be re-learnt and integrated into our everyday world, sprinkling joy and sustenance over all.

Laughter is a joyful embrace of the unexpected, frustrating and glorious. Laughter is a celebration of life. Let's laugh!

laughter
beginnings

Have you ever wondered why we laugh? Laughing is great fun, energising and never fails to grab our attention. It can emerge in gentle chuckles, polite titters or in deep belly guffaws and can change how we feel in an instant. So how did it originate and what happens to us when we laugh?

HOW DID LAUGHTER EVOLVE?

Laughing is an ancient, universal communication tool that has been in existence for at least ten million years. It originated during play within primate groups: today chimpanzees, gorillas, orangutans and bonobos all make laughter sounds when tickled.

Laughter evolved before speech as a way of communicating and strengthening bonds within families of primates. As the sounds developed further, they became a way of 'grooming at a distance' and enhanced the cohesiveness of the community.

Gradually, laughter sounds developed into longer breaths as bipedalism (walking upright) allowed our primate ancestors to stand on two feet, thus freeing the thoracic cavity and enabling them to enjoy greater breath control and acoustic range.

Humans laugh on the outward breath, compared to apes and chimps who laugh with shorter 'panting' breaths, both on the inhale and the exhale. We have developed this elongated 'ha, ha, ha' acoustic exhalation pattern to our laughter structure (unique in the animal kingdom) due to greater freedom of movement of our larynx, thorax and diaphragm.

WHY DID EARLY HUMANS LAUGH?

Another reason our laughter evolved was associated with the relief of tension, worry, anxiety or threat. After a near miss with a dangerous animal our ancestors may have laughed to help release trapped tension in their muscles and skeletal structure.

Primitive laughter also originated in periods of satiation and relaxation, signalling a sense of wellbeing within the group and lengthening periods of play, enjoyment and community. Laughter is a highly contagious activity and our brains respond positively to the sound of laughter, even if we don't actually participate.

Smiling evolved from a need to show others that we were not dangerous: flashing our molars was a way of demonstrating submissiveness and a desire to show allegiance.

LAUGHTER BEFORE HUMOUR

The act of laughing pre-dates humour, which developed much later alongside the evolution of a larger social brain and spoken language. Our ancestors gradually learnt how to punctuate speech sounds with laughter so it became the complex and effective communication tool we use today. Laughter stimulated by jokes became a positive acknowledgement of verbal play amongst humans.

It's highly contagious When we hear or see someone laughing heartily, mirror neurons in our brain prepare our bodies to join in. They activate facial muscles and stimulate involuntary smiles and even real laughter in response.

To communicate affection, connection, love and attention to others Similar to the 'vocal grooming' of our primitive ancestors.

WHY DO WE LAUGH NOWADAYS?

We all laugh for different reasons at different times in our life; here are some of them.

For relief After enduring a challenging experience (e.g. roller coaster ride) we may laugh to release fear or tension that has built up in our minds and bodies.

For fun and enjoyment We can laugh simply to express joy. We experience pleasure, relaxation and a sense of liberation from laughing whether it is voluntary or involuntary.

Out of surprise or humour We may have a set of expectations and when there is a mismatch between these and reality this can result in surprised or sudden laughter (as in jokes and visual humour).

To feel superior to others This usually entails 'laughing at' someone or something. This can be derisive or sarcastic laughter and does not give the same benefits to the laughter as 'laughing with' someone.

Out of choice We can choose to laugh deliberately (voluntary laughter) in order to help both ourselves and others to relax. We may laugh purposefully in order to facilitate communication or to even to enjoy the many health benefits of laughter as a form of exercise.

Why do you like laughing? What does it give you? How did it feel the last time you enjoyed a good belly laugh?

WHAT HAPPENS IN OUR BODIES WHEN WE LAUGH?

Laughing is a genetic, in-built reaction, which usually develops in infants around 3½−4 months of age.
Blind, deaf and sensory impaired children learn to laugh, indicating that laughter is not dependent on the learning environment; it is an innate skill we can all possess.

Laughter is a physiological response that activates a plethora of beneficial reactions in the body. It is a whole body process, which has many benefits for our health and wellbeing.

LAUGHING IS A WHOLE-BODY EXPERIENCE.

BRAIN REACTIONS

When we laugh, a neural electrical response in the brain sends messages to many different areas of the brain (cerebral cortex, pre-frontal lobe, left and right hemispheres, occipital lobe, limbic centre and brain stem) depending on whether the laughter is a response to a joke, humour, event, or a deliberate decision to laugh. The motor regions of the brain also become activated to tell the body to respond in specific ways.

'Always laugh
when you can,
it is cheap
medicine.'

GEORGE GORDON BYRON

The gamma brainwaves produced by extended, hearty laughter are similar to those produced by meditation. These are associated with achieving clarity of the mind and the integration of thoughts. Neurotransmitters, such as endorphins and serotonin are released into the blood stream from neurons in the brain, and these attach themselves onto the 'receptors' of immune cells helping them to adjust their metabolic activity.

MUSCULAR MOVEMENTS

The facial muscles contract and relax, involving both the zygomaticus muscles (the muscles in our cheeks) and the orbicularis oculi muscles (around our eyes) among others. Our faces screw up, our mouth opens and our eyes become half closed or even tight shut. Usually the head tilts back and our faces can turn red due to the increased blood flow and the struggle to catch our breath. The difference in our heart rate and blood pressure causes the capillaries in the skin to dilate and fill with blood, feeding the skin with additional oxygen and nutrients. Our eyes may moisten as the lachrymal gland (which produces tears in our eyes) becomes stimulated.

Muscles in our scalp, neck, arms, back, abdomen, and trunk are exercised, sometimes leaving us 'weak' with laughter. Facial muscles and core muscles in the trunk may tense while others tire, sometimes making it hard to stand up straight or even stay on our feet when we laugh with abandon. The convulsive actions of the muscles help the body to relax and release tension.

BREATHING BONUS

When we laugh our breaths become longer, deeper and more rhythmical as we force more air out and our inhalations lengthen. The lungs work hard to bring in fresh oxygen to the body and to rid the body of stale air and toxins. Laughing exercises the heart, lungs and respiratory system, oxygenating the whole body. Laughter effectively cleanses the respiratory tract, sometimes making us splutter, cough or shift excess mucus in the bronchi as we clear our lungs with breaths of laughter.

ALL PUMPED UP

Our cardiovascular system is activated and the heart pumps faster to cope with the longer breaths, pumping blood faster around the body. Laughter is an aerobic activity that helps the heart and lungs to function efficiently. The inner lining of the blood vessels (the endothelium) expands as we continue to laugh, speeding up blood flow by as much as 22 per cent; this improves circulation and the flow of oxygen to the whole system.

SOUND EXPLOSIONS

The diaphragm and intercostal muscles of the rib cage contract, pushing air out of the lungs in a series of repeated vocal exhalations as the epiglottis half-closes the larynx in the throat, the vocal chords vibrate and air is forced out of a smaller airway. Laughter interrupts speech; we cannot speak coherently and laugh heartily at the same time, although it's very amusing when we try.

LYMPH JOY

The activity of the diaphragm also helps to pump lymph fluid around the body, aiding our lymphatic cleansing system by increasing the movement of lymph by around 15 times the normal rate during a bout of hearty extended laughter. This increased flow of lymph stimulates an increased production of lymphocytes (white blood cells) to help the body stay healthy, thereby strengthening our immune system.

A COCKTAIL OF CHEMICALS

There is also a positive chemical effect in the body. Hormones including endorphins, human growth hormone, serotonin and dopamine are released, helping us to feel good, relax and raise our pain threshold; motivating us to laugh more. Laughter triggers the same reward system in the brain to that triggered by drugs or alcohol (with fewer negative side effects).

Laughter also helps inhibit the production of stress hormones in the body, such as cortisol and epinephrine. As we laugh regularly, more natural killer cells are produced, along with B cells, T cells and antibodies, all of which help to fight infections in the body.

LAUGHING IN 'LAS VAGUS'

As the diaphragm contracts, it massages the internal organs in the body such as the liver, kidneys, ovaries and intestines. It also stimulates the vagus nerve that in turn triggers a relaxation response throughout the body. The autonomic nervous system relaxes with the deeper, longer breaths produced by laughter and this stimulates the calming parasympathetic nervous system (PNS) into action. And there's more…

Recent research studies have found that laughter can lower blood sugar levels and raise good cholesterol levels, because of its effect on heart function and the neuroendocrine system, which monitors glucose levels and hormone production. There has also been encouraging evidence in the last few years regarding the positive effect of laughter in the field of complementary medicine, including treatment of atopic eczema, leg ulcers, depression and infertility. Most of these physiological benefits can be initiated by regular, hearty bouts of joyful laughter, without the need for Lycra. That has to be a bonus.

LAUGHING ON OUR MINDS

Scientific research has now proven that how we think affects the way we feel, and vice versa. This two-way relationship between the mind and the body and how one inextricably affects the other is known as psychoneuroimmunology.

The hormones released into the brain and body when we laugh facilitate relaxation in both areas. This relaxation helps us to let go of things we are worried about, or at least ease their effect on our mental state. When our body is calmed our mind responds likewise. Deep breathing and laughter help us access relaxation and peace, even if it's only for a few minutes. Laughing gives us an important respite in our hectic daily schedule and reminds us that there is more to life than our current mental tussles.

A NEW PAIR OF SPECTACLES

Laughter helps to shift our perspective and creates a little distance between us and our problems, resourcing us with the ability to see difficulties from a different angle; a more subjective viewpoint. It helps us to take 'time out' from the spin of our frenetic daily lives and to have some fun.

Laughter improves our mental functioning as it suppresses the stress hormones and releases relaxing and soothing neurotransmitters. These help to calm us on the inside, give us mental clarity and allow us to think more creatively. When we laugh regularly we are more inclined to take risks, be more adventurous and stay resilient in times of strife. Laughing acts as a brain refresh; helping to improve our memory, concentration and allowing us to approach challenges with renewed energy.

'Laughter is a tranquillizer...

...with no side effects.'

ARNOLD H. GLASOW

POSITIVELY CHARGED

When we laugh we produce more positive thoughts. It is impossible to laugh heartily and feel angry, or to laugh and feel depressed at the same time. Each time we laugh, smile and connect joyfully with one another we are creating new positive neural pathways in the brain, which affect us physically and mentally.

When we think positively we see more possibilities, more opportunities; the world widens in front of our eyes (our peripheral vision literally expands). Laughing helps us to be optimistic, to look for solutions, to become hopeful and happier. It helps us focus on what is going well rather than what has gone wrong. Laughing helps keep us cheerful, even when times get tough.

THE LAUGHTER LEARNING CURVE

Our learning and concentration is improved with laughter – the more we enjoy ourselves, the more deeply we embed our learning. Play, fun and laughter are essential learning components; they make the whole process more memorable, more enjoyable and more effective. Our brains learn better when we are feeling positive, relaxed and energised.

EMOTIONAL TOUGHNESS

Rather than teaching us that life is all about laughing and joyfulness, authentic laughter and experimentation can help us to see laughter as an important tool for coping in stressful times and when life is not going according to plan. We learn through acceptance that the aim is not always to be laughing, but that when we can find a way to laugh it can help ease us into a more resourceful state. Laughter helps us grow strong from the inside out, strengthening our own inner voice, encouraging us to accept the ups and downs of life and to create positive change where needed.

LAUGHTER TOGETHERNESS

Laughter fosters cooperation and team cohesion. It is an instant leveller, demonstrating that we are all the same underneath. Laughing brings people closer together, encouraging trust and openness in group settings. After laughing heartily with someone we feel more inclined to see things from their perspective and to feel empathy, affection and understanding for them.

Laughter creates community and connection. In our modern society, fewer of us live in the type of close-knit communities that were common in the past, and some of us live isolated and independent lives, with little or no regular contact with other people. Loneliness is the scourge of our current times and is very much prevalent in all areas of the world. We all need a sense of belonging and connection with other people; we are social creatures and not designed to live or function on our own for long periods of time. Laughter can help us feel connected to others and to bring us into contact with them in a joyful and meaningful way. Laughing in a supportive group atmosphere helps us to stay healthy and resilient, to enjoy life to the full and to experience a sense of purpose.

PRESENT MOMENT IMMERSION

There is an unlimited ocean of peace in every moment if we allow ourselves to fully let go in mind and body. Laughing is like being plunged into the depths of the present moment in glorious technicolour. Our senses become heightened as we experience viscerally the sheer delight of laughter and let it take the reins; guiding us to an unknown place. Through embracing laughter we learn that although we cannot control what happens in life,

WE CAN CONTROL HOW WE RESPOND TO WHAT HAPPENS...

CREATIVE EXPRESSION

Laughter helps us to express delight, playfulness, celebration, relief, unity, joy, gratitude, ecstasy, love, humour, a sense of wellbeing, triumph, happiness and many other positive emotions. It can also create a breathing space in times of tension or anxiety, such as at funerals or when visiting those who are unwell. It acts as a reliever, a comforter and an energy booster.

So what do we need in order to let go and laugh...?

'With mirth and laughter let old wrinkles come.'

WILLIAM SHAKESPEARE

laughter
readiness

Are you ready to laugh?

Laughter requires so little
from us and gives us so much in
return. However there are many, many
people in the world who haven't laughed
in a really long time or who struggle to laugh
at all. Laughter is a choice. However before we can
choose laughter, there may be some existing beliefs
and assumptions we need to question first. These limiting
beliefs can prevent us from allowing ourselves to become
relaxed and immersed in the laughter process.

LAUGHTER MYTHS

There are some myths about laughing which are not obvious but can affect how we think, feel and behave when it comes to letting go and enjoying a good belly laugh.

MYTH 1

We must be happy in order to laugh.

This myth inhibits many people from laughing as they feel that it would be inauthentic or 'false' to laugh when they didn't feel like it. If we wait for the perfect time to laugh, or wait for everything in life to be running smoothly we may never laugh at all! Laughter can surprise us and offer relief in times of turmoil, sadness or even grief, if we allow it to.

LAUGHING MAKES US FEEL BETTER; IT'S AS SIMPLE AS THAT.

Can you remember a time when you were feeling terrible and someone or something made you laugh despite yourself and you felt better for it?

MYTH 2

We need something funny to happen before we can laugh.

Comedy is great and can be the trigger for many a hearty chortle. Yet evidence shows that the majority of our laughter doesn't come from jokes; it comes from day to day conversations and playfulness. If we wait for something funny to happen we may wait for a really long time. Laughter is too good to leave to chance. Laughter is not a passive activity; it is a 'total immersion, commitment to everyday happiness' type of process. If we want to enjoy life to the full, we need to make our own happiness as we travel rather than wait for the entertainment bus to show up.

LAUGHTER IS NOT A COMPETITION.

MYTH 3

We have either a natural propensity to laugh or not.

It doesn't matter if you are a shy or introverted person or if you haven't laughed for a really long time. It's not about who can laugh the longest, loudest or heartiest. It doesn't matter if you feel you have lost your ability to laugh or you can't remember the last time you laughed. The good news is that laughter is accessible to us all. It is a re-learnable skill that can be re-acquired, one chuckle at a time.

THREE KEYS TO LAUGHING MORE

So what do we need in order to laugh? A mouth comes in very handy, but there are also three important keys to laughing more:

1. UNDERSTANDING HOW LAUGHTER CAN HELP US

As demonstrated in chapter one, laughter can help us mentally, physically, socially and emotionally in many different ways. Laughter is not just for fun (though that's a huge reason!); it is a healthy, natural tool that can ease our pain, free our spirit and strengthen us from the inside out.

2. BEING WILLING TO LAUGH

Willingness is essential as it provides powerful energy in our mind, body and soul. If we nurture a laughter intention as we go through life this will enable us to feel lighter, stay playful and look on the bright side instead of focusing on what has gone wrong. Being willing to laugh takes us halfway there.

What does laughter give you? Imagine laughing freely and easily whenever you want to. What difference would that make in your life?

3. GIVING OURSELVES PERMISSION TO LAUGH

We are allowed to laugh whenever we want. We don't have to deserve it. We don't need to have done something 'right' or 'worthy'. We don't need to be feeling joyful or happy. If we can stop putting conditions on our laughter then we can access laughter at any time of day or night, if we so choose. We don't always need to laugh in the same way, or with particular people or in certain locations. Our laughter doesn't have to be real, or loud, or demanding. By gently dissolving the traditional and limiting beliefs associated with laughing we can open up the parameters of our laughter to discover new realms of freedom and adventure. Giving ourselves permission to laugh messily, clumsily, noisily, ridiculously, silently and for no apparent reason other than it feels good, may be a great place to start.

Are you willing to laugh? What stops you from laughing? How encouraging are you of your own happiness? Are you ready to accept your laughter no matter what it sounds like?

COMMON LAUGHTER FEARS

Many people are self-conscious or embarrassed to laugh out loud in company; here are some frequently heard worries.

'MY TEETH ARE UNEVEN, I FEEL SO SELF-CONSCIOUS.'

Laughter is not about being perfect – it is quite the opposite. It is about accepting our faults, embracing our shortcomings and loving ourselves unconditionally. When we laugh with people we trust, we allow ourselves to be vulnerable – teeth and all! – to find that laughter is not about surface effects or comparisons, but about heart-to-heart connections. When we laugh with another person, we connect through our eyes, which are usually shining, bright and alive with joy. Our face softens, colour comes to our cheeks and we are at our most natural. We never look as beautiful as when we smile and laugh. Allow your thoughts about what people are thinking to be positive ones. Assume the best of others, not the worst. Laughing freely helps us to build trust in ourselves and in others.

'I LEAD A HUGE TEAM AND HAVE TO BE PROFESSIONAL. I DON'T WANT TO LOSE CONTROL.'

We can be professional and have fun at the same time. Being a strong, inspirational leader is not all about control and efficiency; it is about enabling others to be the best they can be. Allowing ourselves the opportunity to laugh, play and relax at work encourages others to do the same. When we are relaxed and happy we all perform at our best.

'IF I START TO LAUGH I MIGHT CRY...'

Yes you might, and what is the harm in that? Both tears and laughter can act as a means of catharsis for pent-up feelings and emotions to surface. When we manage to release these emotions we often feel a sense of lightness, increased freedom and renewed energy. Giving yourself a loving, safe space to explore these hidden feelings may help you to move forward with issues that have previously held you back. Sometimes we need to cry before we can laugh, and vice versa. Please seek advice from a trained counsellor or medical practitioner if needed.

'I DON'T WANT TO APPEAR SILLY OR RIDICULOUS. PEOPLE WILL THINK I AM CRAZY.'

If we worry constantly about what other people think then we will start to live our lives to please others rather than listening to our own desires. We are never going to please everyone and it can feel exhausting even to try.

Don't be afraid of being silly; 'silly' comes from the ancient English phrase 'gesaelig', meaning 'blessed, prosperous and happy'. Children are silly and playful and generally laugh a great deal more than adults. Silliness is a liberating, creative state that re-energises and frees us from our habits and routines. We need to start embracing being silly, one tiny step (tippy toe) at a time.

To help lubricate the whole LAUGH process there are luckily some stabling, supportive elements to the whole laughter landscape that we can utilise…

What would you like to have happen? When was the last time you were silly? How did that feel?

'At the height of laughter

the Universe

is flung

into a kaleidoscope

of new possibilities.'

JEAN HOUSTON

ELEVEN LAUGHTER LOOSENERS

The following qualities or traits are useful laughter partners. These elements facilitate the flow of laughter in our everyday life, and support and encourage us in the process.

PURPOSE

We need to understand why laughter is so useful and most importantly, know why it is important to us. If you could create a vision or symbol for your life with more laughter in it, what would it look like? What would that give you? This is your WHY. Draw or record it (in colour if you feel the urge) as a reminder and motivator for those days when you find it hard to laugh.

PLAYFULNESS

Allowing yourself to be playful is an extraordinary way of being that enables us to see possibilities, humour and adventure in the ordinary. Playing encourages us to dig deep for the funny, to explore uncharted waters, to take risks and lose ourselves blissfully in the present moment. When we are being playful we stretch our imagination to the sky and back; expanding our creative horizons. (And that's where all the fun is.)

PRESENT MOMENT AWARENESS (PMA) OR MINDFULNESS

Paying attention to the present moment, noticing the small details as well as the bigger picture, is a skill much needed in today's society. Mindfulness enables us to focus where otherwise we might be full of assumptions. Mindfulness trains our senses to work at their optimum, enhancing everyday life. If we learn to pause in our daily swirl of activities and become fully present to whatever is happening at that moment, we will be able to pause and laugh easily. Laughter is mindfulness in motion.

CURIOSITY

One of life's greatest joys is to wonder, question and explore. Look intently for the unusual, novel and ridiculous. Curiosity opens us up to impossible possibilities. Curiosity encourages us to embrace the unknown even in frustrating circumstances and persevere when we might have given up.

CONNECTION

We are 30 times more likely to laugh with other people than on our own. As we are social creatures we benefit from regular, supportive interactions with others, particularly if they are positive and fun-loving. Strengthening these relationships and building new ones aids the laughter process.

OPTIMISM

Having the attitude of 'glass half full' rather than 'glass half empty' enables us to embrace life. If we produce more positive thoughts than unhelpful ones, we seek out the joys and look for things that amuse us. Laughing and optimism dance hand in hand, complementing one another and creating some beautiful shapes together.

GRATITUDE

Often we forget the many small things there are to be grateful for. Practising gratitude frequently is a fast track to happiness and reminds us how lucky we are. Gratitude makes it even easier to smile and laugh. Laughing helps us to feel grateful and vibrant, and in turn being grateful enables us to play and laugh more easily.

COURAGE

To laugh with no obvious reason, to play because we feel the urge – these actions are considered the antithesis of a normal, sane existence in the 21st century. Yet people everywhere in the modern world are mentally suffocating in stress-filled schedules, experiencing little or no relaxation every day. It takes courage to make a stand and show through our actions that playfulness and laughter are not only crucial for our health and wellbeing, the world is a lonelier, sadder place without it.

COMMITMENT

Dedicating ourselves to sharing joy, laughter and fun with others is a passionate pilgrimage, and one that also requires daily practice and continued effort. Staying optimistic, playful and open to laughter requires patience, commitment and consistency, especially on days when things are falling apart at the seams.

ACCEPTANCE

We all benefit from positive reinforcement when learning. Laughing is no exception. Having a deep sense of self-respect and self-compassion is paramount to learning how we can let go and laugh. If we can be kind and generous to ourselves in our thoughts and actions then the whole process will flow more easily and enjoyably. We cannot laugh freely if we are demanding or self-critical.

SURRENDER

Relinquishing control is a pre-requisite to laughing freely. Laughter flows from trust, openness and surrender. When we laugh uncontrollably we let go, opening ourselves to the unknown and embracing the moment. When we hold on to being 'in control', our laughter is restricted. Surrender comes with a deep-seated trust in the laughter process. This can be nurtured with patience and understanding.

TUNING INTO LAUGHTER

The aspects of life we pay the most attention to are the ones that are likely to expand and strengthen. When we open up the filters of our mind to laughter possibilities we notice more of them. Tuning into laughter is like tuning our 'mind radio' to the laughter frequency; our awareness widens and attracts more laughter to us. We start to discover it in simple, everyday things.

ENERGY FLOWS WHERE OUR ATTENTION GOES.

BEGIN BY NOTICING LAUGHTER AROUND YOU

This could be on the radio, TV, Internet, in conversations with people, in cafés, at work – even waiting for the bus.

START TO COLLECT YOUR FUNNY

What sorts of interactions, events and experiences make you want to smile or laugh? It doesn't matter at this stage whether you are just smiling or laughing out loud, just begin to notice where and when you smile or laugh, where the laughter starts and who you are with.

'From there to here, from here to there, funny things are everywhere.'

DR. SEUSS

TUNING INTO LAUGHTER
COULD INCLUDE:

Starting a laughter log, either in a file or folder on the computer or in a scrapbook or diary so you can record smiles and laughs as they arise.

Noticing laughs, banter or teasing in **conversations** that you overhear or that you participate in.

Listening to the **radio, TV or Internet,** jotting down things you found amusing or entertaining.

Counting how many **smiles** you give or receive during the day.

Recording **laughter memories** from the past, when, where and with whom.

Making a **list of people** you find it easy to laugh with, now or in the past.

Making a **list of comedy shows** you enjoy and watch them again.

Writing down a list of **games, stories, songs, films, plays, poetry or books** you have enjoyed that made you laugh.

Accepting that you may not be smiling or laughing much at the moment and that is fine.

Writing down any **'laughter triggers'**, things that make you instantly smile or laugh.

Keeping a folder of internet jokes, videos or interviews that make you smile or laugh.

Recording **playful times** you experience or have enjoyed in the past.

Making a list of **mistakes or embarrassing moments** that you have managed to laugh about.

Cutting out **cartoons, jokes, photos or pictures** that make you smile or laugh.

Draw a **laughter chart** to plot on the high points and low points of laughter throughout your life so far to see where you laughed the most and what helped you.

Noticing the **urge to smile or laugh**.

Spending free time with **young children or animals**.

Noticing the **different types of laughter** experienced and how you felt before, during and afterwards.

Creating a **laughter map** with times, events, people, situations and places that made you laugh.

'I grew up with six brothers. That's how I learnt to dance – waiting for the bathroom.'

BOB HOPE

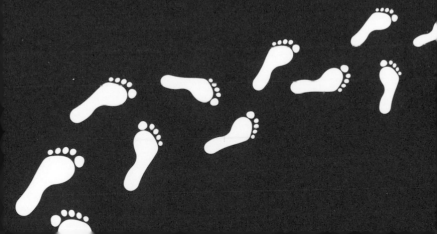

laughter
innovation

We are the co-creators
of our existence. With
our thoughts, beliefs and
actions we create our world.

Watching comedy and listening to
humour are great pastimes and they
can be wonderful stimulants for laughter,
especially when shared with loved ones. However
finding the 'right' humour for us can be tricky... and
saving our laughs for comedy shows or jokes means
that our laughter can become passive – reliant on
the existence of jokes, comedy or humour of others.
Waiting for laughs to come our way is like waiting
for a bus: we could be sitting around for ages, it may
be cancelled at any time and it may be headed in
one direction when we want to go in the other.

LETTING OURSELVES OUT TO PLAY

Choosing to adopt a playful attitude is the first step to laughing.

PLAYING MEANS THERE ARE NO RIGHT ANSWERS

The world becomes a place of exploration and discovery. Creating laughs where there were none means letting go of the outcome, paying attention to our bodies, our breathing, how we feel and the world around us. Playing connects us to the present moment without conditions. It is a liberation of the soul, leading us from the concrete into the vast wilderness of the imagination.

PLAYING WITH LAUGHTER MEANS EXPERIMENTING

Making mistakes, questioning, trialling, moulding and sculpting, arranging and re-arranging. Playing with laughter means that we can accept our right to laugh messily, uncontrollably, squeakily, irresponsibly... unconditionally.

What if we could discover more play, fun and laughter in everyday life?

EXPLORE, EXPERIMENT AND TRY OUT LAUGHS

Do it just for the sake of laughing, because it feels good and does us good. We can learn to love our laugh, however it sounds (and it will sound different each day).

NOTICE WHAT MAKES US FEEL JOYFUL

Being aware of shifts in our bodies during the day and paying attention to when we feel lighter, springier and free.

What if we could create laughter opportunities for ourselves?

LAUGHTER INNOVATION

Means laughing from the inside out, choosing to laugh rather than waiting for the right external circumstances to be met. Deep happiness comes from within.

BEING PLAYFUL MEANS TRYING NEW THINGS

Stepping out of the safe harbour and making waves in an uncharted ocean. If we think we might look silly… then who is thinking that? Is it our critical self who wants us to be sensible and safe or our lighter, naturally playful, inquisitive self?

What if we could laugh because we choose to?

WEARING PLAY GOGGLES

Laughter emerges naturally out of play. Being willing to play lightens our whole world. When we can allow ourselves to be playful we may find laughter happens inexplicably. Imagine the world as a three-year-old.

What might you try? How would you move? What would you be interested in?

We are certainly not all extroverts and some of us purposefully shy away from the limelight. So we can experiment and play on our own to begin with. It doesn't matter if we don't laugh out loud, smile or even find playing hysterically funny, it just matters that we start.

What is enjoyable? Where do you find yourself totally absorbed? Can you allow yourself the freedom to 'be silly'?

'Play is the highest form of research.'

ALBERT EINSTEIN

SOME LIGHT LAUGHTER STARTERS

Try some of the following movements and activities in odd moments to see how your body and mind feel:

PRETENDING,
IMAGINING,
DAYDREAMING,
EXPLORING

SKIPPING,
STEPPING
GRANDLY,
TIPTOEING,
SHUFFLING

BUILDING, STICKING,
FOLDING, PATTING

DRESSING UP, COLOURING,
DOODLING, SCRIBBLING

DANCING,
STOMPING,
ROLLING,
CLIMBING

NOISE MAKING,
MUSIC MAKING,
SINGING,
WHISTLING

These experiments may lead to laughter, they may not. We are creating laughter opportunities. We are saying **'YES'** to embracing what is inside and around us. We are forging connections. We are beginning to make friends with the present moment.

DO THE UNEXPECTED. LOOK FOR THE INVISIBLE. DARE YOURSELF. FOLLOW THOSE URGES...

HIDING, SURPRISING, FINDING, HUGGING

JUMPING, SLIDING, CREEPING, MARCHING

FACE PULLING, WRIGGLING, SQUEEZING, HOLDING

PUSHING, TUGGING, TEASING, WRESTLING

GARGLING, YODELLING, SPLASHING, JIGGLING

LOOSENING THE BODY LOOSENS THE MIND

It's hard to have fun when we feel lethargic, restricted or tense in our body. Loosening our body loosens our mind and loosens our laughter. Loosening the body, how we walk, how we move and how we breathe means that we can have fun whenever we want and we require no special equipment or resources. Go gently and listen to your body, and vary these exercises as you need to.

BODY BOOSTERS

Try some of the following for starters and add your own inventive ideas:

Faces
Pulling faces, gurning, eyebrow dancing, ear wiggling, nostril flaring, cheek squashing, touching your nose with your tongue, making popping sounds with your fingers and your cheeks, making animal faces.

Feet and Legs Roller skating, striding, clip-clopping, trundling, stamping, walking between the cracks in the pavement, balancing, bounding, side stepping, weaving, walking backwards, leaping, dodging, high stepping, shuffling, prancing, stomping, jumping, stepping, skipping.

Hands and arms Clapping, tapping, clicking fingers, finger dancing, thumb twiddling, thumb wrestling, poking, flicking, rolling, conducting, gesticulating, finger drumming, patting, scooping, waving, signalling, beckoning, moulding, sculpting, weaving, crocheting, drawing, doodling, cartooning, gluing, sticking, painting, splashing, squashing, digging, pummelling, smoothing, stroking, touching, holding, squeezing, pointing, swinging, shaking, prodding.

Games Tag, 'IT', sardines, hide and seek, circle games, made-up games.

Word play Making up rhymes for everyday objects, using foreign accents, silly voices, creating puns, talking in a nonsense, made-up language.

Funky movements Wiggling, jiggling, sliding, crawling, swerving, dodging, twirling, swaying, galloping.

Funny noises Gulping, slurping, screeching, sucking, hissing, sighing, blowing raspberries, tutting, making a horse cantering sound, saying 'wheee', yodelling, practising scales, making up imaginary sounds for everyday objects, Tarzan calls, beat boxing.

Dancing Inventing your own style of tango, flamenco, ballroom, tap dancing, jigging, beat boxing, belly dancing, ballet, Morris dancing, disco, hip hop.

Singing Loudly, quietly, suspiciously, mysteriously, angrily, dramatically, tunelessly, passionately, silently, duets, solos, harmonies.

Teasing See Tickling.

Tickling NOTE Only to be practised with people you are close to and who like to be tickled, and obviously only if you like being tickled yourself.

Wrestling See Tickling.

Mimes Create your own silent actions and gestures, use the power of silence and fun to convey what you want to say.

Improvisation Play out different scenarios and unlikely situations with ridiculous themes, characters, voices and props.

Joke telling and listening Learn some jokes, tell them, retell them, change them, listen to them, share them, make them up, record them, tell good ones, corny ones… and laugh anyway.

'A person who
knows how
to laugh at
himself will
never cease to
be amused.'

SHIRLEY MACLAINE

LAUGHING AT OURSELVES

Playing encourages us to lighten up and to stop taking ourselves quite so seriously; it invites us to see life as a game and an adventure, an open door. We start to see ourselves as playing parts or roles in the game. We see our mistakes, blunders and mishaps as part of the whole process, to be forgiven and accepted with love and humour. Our mistakes remind us of our infallibility, our imperfections and our humanness.

LAUGHING AT OURSELVES SETS US FREE.

TEN WAYS TO LAUGH AT YOURSELF

1. **Smile at your messy image** in the mirror first thing in the morning – the messier the better.

2. **Laugh when you make a mistake** and tell someone about it.

3. **Notice when you are trying too hard in life**, love yourself for it, then smile and sigh loudly to relax.

4. **Exaggerate your worst traits and habits…** play with them, bring them out into the light.

5. **Find a sign to put over your desk** that makes you laugh.

6. **Spend time with a friend or relative** who can tease you, laugh with you and encourage you to let go.

7. **Blow a huge, messy and loud raspberry** whenever you need a bit of fast, light relief.

8. **Create a light-hearted alter ego for yourself** and secretly give yourself a name and a character of someone who takes things less seriously – it could be 'Disastrous Delilah' or 'Ridiculous Robert', and imagine how they would respond. *What would they do? How would they think and behave?*

9. **Sing about how you feel in the moment**, as loudly and tunelessly as possible.

10. **Announce a headline or key phrase in a solemn tone** for over-serious moments, for example, 'this is Sally Serious, reporting for Deadly Serious News at Ten.'

LAUGHING WITH OTHERS

Laughter is a social tool; we usually laugh most when we are with other people. So it's vital to find some like-minded, fun loving, trusted friends or family to laugh with. Finding and making friends with people who can be playful, silly and non-judgemental is imperative to laughing frequently and freely.

LAUGHTER LINKS

Having one laughter mate who you can pick up the phone and instantly laugh with is a precious gift. Finding a group of people with whom you can laugh unconditionally is a treasure trove.

Relationships are strengthened and forged with authenticity, vulnerability and trust. Laughter relationships can be cemented in a few minutes, or sculpted over several years; they all require thoughtfulness and effort to be maintained. Luckily, the relationship wheel can be liberally oiled with laughter.

The more open-hearted, playful and authentic we can be, the better our relationships. Staying open to laughter in any relationship is possible, and if shared laughter emerges it can instantly break down any barriers. The more we laugh with others, the closer we feel to them and vice versa.

BUILDING OUR OWN LAUGHTER NETWORK IS VITAL TO CONTINUED LAUGHTER PRACTICE AND A RICH LIFE.

SONGS, MUSIC AND DANCING

Light-hearted music is a great catalyst for laughter when we immerse ourselves in it. Try some of the following:

Making up your own raps, ditties and lyrics about everyday objects e.g. 'Rock and Roll Loo Roll' or 'Dishcloths I have loved and lost'.

Trying one of these: belly dancing, limbo in the garden, whistling or humming a tune for others to guess, singing at the top of your voice or impersonating your favourite or worst singer.

Imagining you are a professional ballet dancer, keyboard player, or rap artist and twirl or stomp enthusiastically.

Making an ensemble with some friends, for example, singing about your local pub, living in your home town or catching a cold.

Bringing ordinary objects alive with a song and dance number, such as mops, spoons or paper clips.

Creating a percussion band out of objects in your desk or your living room and singing to accompany the noise.

Dancing ridiculously to a type of music you would never usually play.

Doing some kitchen karaoke improvising a song about the meal you are cooking in the kitchen and juggling with the fruit in the fruit bowl.

Drumming but if no drums are available, use your body and clap or drum a rhythm using your hands or legs.

Conducting enthusiastically with a range of different household or office implements.

Dancing the conga with people in your bus queue or with people in your office.

PLAYFUL PAIRED CHALLENGES

Find out who can...

Stay serious for the longest

Gargle the loudest

Thumb wrestle, arm wrestle or tummy wrestle the best

Walk the silliest walk

Sing the highest note

Cram the most grapes in their mouth

Pull the worst face

Tell the corniest joke

Stand up straight balancing on one leg while someone else tries to make them wobble

Play 'knee tag'

Say a tongue-twister the fastest

Answer the phone with the poshest voice

Invent the most puns

SAVOURING THE MOMENT

Wherever you are, pay close attention to what is going on. Use your senses and notice feelings, sensations, sounds, sights, smells and even tastes. Be interested in all of it. Look carefully at details and the whole picture. Choose what you are most drawn to. Re-connect repeatedly with your inner child throughout the day and ask yourself questions like:

How could this be more fun?

If I was being playful right now what would that be like?

What is the playful clown in me noticing right now?

gentle laughter

We do not always have to be laughing loudly or heartily. You may be already laughing frequently or you may not have laughed at all in the last few years; either way it is always good to learn to laugh gently. It's a bit like going for a run; you wouldn't usually sprint out the door straight away, you would probably stretch, walk or jog slowly at first. Treating ourselves kindly and gently in life is paramount for an enjoyable existence, and learning to laugh gently mirrors this practice.

STARTING WITH A SMILE

SMILING LAYS DOWN A WELCOME MAT FOR LAUGHTER.

Smiling activates a place in the brain called the orbitofrontal cortex so that even if we merely think about someone smiling we want to smile. A simple smile releases the feel-good hormones endorphins, serotonin and dopamine and lights us up from the inside.

A smile is a heartfelt connection; a silent gesture that helps to close the distance between two people. It is a clear message of peace and signals friendliness, openness and a willingness to trust. When our smile is genuine we reveal our true nature.

Even when enduring a stressful experience, the physical act of smiling can help us to let go of tension, to feel more relaxed and to recover more quickly after the event.

Smiling is so simple and easy to do that we often underplay the powerful impact it can have on our emotional and physical health.

SMILE FACTS

- A genuine smile is also known as the 'Duchenne' smile when it reaches and engages the muscles around the eyes (their Latin name is orbicularis oculi) as well as the muscles around the mouth (zygomaticus major).

- Smiling can use between five and 53 muscles, depending how wide your grin is.

- Babies have been recorded smiling in the womb.

- Smiling is the most easily recognised facial expression and can be identified up to 300ft (91.5m) away.

- Smiling is contagious; it fires off mirror neurones in our brains that make us mimic what we are seeing in someone else's face.

- Smiling lowers our heart rate and blood pressure and relaxes our body.

- Smiling melts resistance, encourages patience and eases us into the flow of life.

SMILING CHANGES OUR INTERNAL AND EXTERNAL EXPERIENCE OF THE WORLD.

SMILING EXERCISES

Every day, **TRY SMILING AT YOURSELF IN THE MIRROR**.

START AND FINISH YOUR DAY WITH A SMILE, let the smile remind you of the good in your life.

SMILE AT ANYONE: try smiling at people who are not smiling and people who are already smiling.

BE BRAVE AND KEEP EYE CONTACT AS YOU SMILE, really notice what happens in people's eyes when they smile at you.

NOTICE SMILES AROUND YOU; collect memories of smiles like you are etching them on your brain.

PRACTISE SMILING even when there is nothing to smile about.

PRACTISE FAKE SMILING AND REAL SMILING so you get to know how each one feels.

PLAY WITH DIFFERENT SMILES; try a saucy smile, a sinister smile, a cheesy smile…

PRACTISE SMILING OUTWARDLY, THEN INWARDLY without showing the smile on your face, imagine your whole body is smiling and notice what happens.

ALLOW YOURSELF TO SMILE when you feel stressed, or angry, or tense and worried.

BREATHE DEEPLY WHEN YOU SMILE, really savour how it feels in your body, what do you notice?

SMILE AT OTHERS WITH NO EXPECTATION of a smile in return.

GENTLE LAUGHTER STARTER EXERCISES

GENERAL GUIDELINES

Go gently, listen to your body, there should be no new pain and never force your laughter. Keep these exercises short and frequent, no longer than a few seconds to begin with. Have fun with them! Start just with smiling and allow a few chuckles (gentle laughs) to emerge given time and practice. It is common to start coughing as your airways start to clear. This is normal; remember to drink plenty of water before and afterwards. **Rest as much as you need and adapt the exercises to suit you.** It is also common to experience yawning, which helps you to release tension and enables you to relax. You may want to do these exercises either on your own in a secluded place to begin with or alongside a willing laughter partner from the very start.

NOTE
Before undertaking any new exercise it is advisable to check with your doctor. Please look at the contra-indicators for laughter in the Safety Notes on pages 140–141 of this book.

'A laugh is
a smile that
bursts.'

MARY H. WALDRIP

BREATHE, STRETCH, SMILE

Sit or stand alert and relaxed. Breathe in deeply as you raise your arms above your head, hold for a second, then lower and smile as you exhale. Now repeat, inhaling and stretching with your arms or legs in any direction that feels comfortable or fun, then exhale deeply, remembering to smile and relax. Get creative with your stretches, let out a gentle chuckle with the exhale if you feel one emerging.

FACIAL BREATHING

Have fun with breathing; inhale and exhale whilst pulling different faces looking at a partner or at yourself in the mirror. You can use your hands to help your face contort as you inhale and exhale.

EXAGGERATED YAWNING

Yawns are a great way to release tension and involve an intake of healthy oxygen, so we may as well enjoy the process. Next time you feel a yawn coming on, really exaggerate the movement and the sound, luxuriate in the full pleasure of the yawn and finish with a smile and a sigh.

SMILE, RISE AND SIGH

Stand firmly on the ground with your feet a hip's width apart and your arms by your sides. Fix your attention on the area just below your belly button, breathe slowly and imagine a smile in your stomach. Connect with this smile and imagine it spreading down your legs to your toes as you carry on breathing. Visualise smiles on the soles of your feet. Breathe in and rise up on your tiptoes, bringing your arms up as high as you feel comfortable doing and smiling at the same time. Lower your arms and feet slowly with an audible sigh. Repeat, the sigh – 'haaaaa' – gently as you return your arms and feet to their starting position. Stand still and imagine a smile somewhere in your body.

OPERATIC BREATHING

Breathe with exaggerated expression and feeling, as if performing in an opera, wave your arms about gently in rhythm with your breathing. Smile broadly and savour each gorgeous intake of oxygen and smile, feeling it nourish your body. Make a loud sigh or musical note on the exhale. Imagine this is the most wonderful breath you have taken today.

'Every time
you smile
at someone,

it is an action
of love, a gift to
that person,

a beautiful
thing.'

MOTHER TERESA

HUGGING LAUGH

Hug yourself (or someone else – with their permission) gently and smile as you start to rock your body softly. When it begins to feel good and you notice yourself beginning to relax, start to laugh gently and kindly.

SUPERHERO SMILE

Imagine you are wearing a colourful cape and have been summoned to do something extraordinary like saving the Universe before lunch. Stand or sit magnificently, toss your imaginary cape over your shoulders, breathe, smile and release a loud and defiant 'Ha'. Repeat, followed by a 'Ha, ha, ha' in exaggerated, superhero style, and then stride around, still declaring 'Ha, ha, ha' in a heroic fashion.

PATTED LAUGH

Step one: begin by patting your body slowly all over with short little laughter sounds ('Ha, ha, ha, ha') to wake yourself up, then pause, breathe and smile. Step two: speed up the patting before you rest, breathe and smile for a second time. Step three: pat and laugh really fast for a couple of seconds, anywhere you want. Repeat these three steps with different laughter sounds.

PLAYING WITH LAUGHTER SOUNDS

There are many laughter sounds that are located in various places in the body. After a while you will find more and more of your own and will be able to blend these naturally together in real laughter as it emerges. We have outlined a few key laughter sounds for you to play with as a starting point. You can access these sounds easily with willingness, playfulness and experimentation. (Practise on your own or with a willing partner; you can sit facing each other and using playful eye contact or lying side by side on the floor.)

IMPORTANT NOTE
THESE LAUGHTER SOUNDS DO NOT NEED TO SOUND AUTHENTIC OR REMOTELY LIKE REAL LAUGHTER – YOU CAN JUST PLAY WITH THEM, ADAPT THEM AND USE THEM TO FIND OUT WHAT FEELS GOOD FOR YOU. THE BODY CANNOT DISTINGUISH BETWEEN A REAL LAUGH AND A SIMULATED ONE SO YOU RECEIVE ALL THE PHYSIOLOGICAL BENEFITS OF A REAL LAUGH EVEN IF YOU 'PRETEND LAUGH' TO BEGIN WITH.

BELLY LAUGH HO, HO, HO, HO, HO

Sit or stand comfortably but alert. Hold your arms out to the sides of your body, inhale deeply, move your hands to your lower belly and hold. Imagine laughter building up inside. Slowly release your hands outwards as you make as many 'Ho, ho, ho, ho, ho' sounds on the exhalation as you like, imagining the laughter emerging from your belly button.

Imagine what colour your laughter could be and where it could go.

RIBCAGE LAUGH HU, HU, HU, HU, HU

Hold your arms out to the sides, take a deep breath in as you move your hands to the lower ribcage area; keep your hands there as you hold your breath for a second. Feel the laughter build then make 'Hu, hu, hu, hu, hu' sounds as you exhale, opening your arms outwards, imagining the laughter is coming out of your ribcage as your hands move apart. Repeat and experiment, adapting as you go to help the laughter flow.

Take long, slow, calm breaths in between these exercises to re-balance, rest and still your body. You can smile gently.

HEARTY LAUGH
HA, HA, HA, HA, HA

Hold your arms out to the sides of your body, take a deep breath in as you move your hands towards your heart and rest them there. Hold your breath and smile for a second, imagining a deep laugh in the centre of your heart. Fling your arms outwards on the exhale and make 'Ha, ha, ha, ha, ha' sounds (opening your mouth wider here may help the laughter to escape). You can tilt your head back if it's comfortable for you. Repeat as many times as you like, changing the volume, the pitch, the speed and the direction of your laugh, and then rest and smile.

THROATY LAUGH
HEE, HEE, HEE, HEE, HEE

Place one hand gently on your throat and imagine a smile there. With your fingers gently touching your throat so you can feel the vibrations, gently make the laughter sounds 'Hee, hee, hee, hee, hee' in your throat, looking in the mirror or into another person's eyes. Repeat a few times if you like the way it feels.

GOOD VIBRATIONS

You can sit, stand or lie down for this exercise; whichever is easiest for you. Choose a point on your body and rest your hands on this area, close your eyes, breathe and smile. Imagine a laugh waiting there, ready to play. Take a deep breath in (keeping your hands on your body if it's comfortable to feel the vibrations), hold your breath for a second, and then make laughter sounds on the exhale that you think might come from this area. Explore, extend or shorten the laughs, breathe and continue to make as many laughter sounds as you like. Rest and breathe slowly, wait for your heart to settle. Then laugh again from another point on your body. You can move the body part with your hands as you laugh if it helps you to laugh more freely.

VISUALISE THE LAUGHTER

Try laughing with your feet, your knees, your hips, tummy, chest, arms, hands, fingers, head, brain... it's your body and your imagination! Add movements to accompany the laughter as required. Visualise the laughter travelling around your whole body, spreading joy, wellbeing and relaxation to every cell.

KEEP CHECKING IN AND NOTICING WHEN YOUR LAUGHTER FEELS GOOD.

POSSIBLE LAUGHTER VARIATIONS

Movements Laughing whilst walking, running, gardening, cleaning or keeping still.

Position Laughing when sitting, standing, lying down, sitting on floor with knees bent.

Volume Laughing silently, quietly, gently, loudly, raucously, close-mouthed, open-mouthed.

Place Laughing outside, indoors, lying in bed, sitting on the floor, a chair or on a beanbag, in front of a mirror, under a tree.

What kind of laughter do you enjoy most? What kind of laughter do you find easiest to create? What helps you to let go and laugh in these exercises? Are you being encouraging to yourself?

Your body is unique and it is important that you find ways to laugh that feel wonderful for you.

Sometimes these laughter exercises will give way to natural, free laughter and at other times they won't. Accept all of this, it is part of the laughter process. **Remember how even simulated laughter helps our bodies to release stress, re-energise and relax.**

People Laughing on your own, with one other person or with several people.

Eyes Open or closed.

Timing Laughing first thing in the morning, during the day, at night-time.

Duration Laughing with shorter sounds, longer sounds, changing the pace and rhythm.

TYPES OF LAUGHS

Play with different laughs to see how they feel.

CACKLY

COURAGEOUS

UNCONTROLLABLE

SUPERIOR

POLITE

RELUCTANT

ANGRY

CHUCKLY

EXPLOSIVE

STIFLED

GENTLE

CHEEKY

CHERISH YOUR LAUGH AT ALL TIMES. IT IS AN EXPRESSION OF YOU.

PAIRED LAUGHTER EXERCISES

Laughter as a shared experience allows us to connect deeply with another person and to break down the barriers of self-consciousness. Here are some exercises to try.

Laughter putty Pass a piece of pretend stretchy laughter putty between you both, creating your own laughter sounds as the putty changes shape.

Forbidden laugh Sit quietly facing each other, eye contact is allowed but no smiling. Make creative sounds to one another – no laughing allowed.

Laughter crescendo One person starts to laugh very quietly in a particular way, the other copies it but more loudly… pass the laugh backwards and forwards increasing the volume until one person decides it's too loud and begins a new, different laugh really quietly. Repeat.

Embarrassed laugh Share an 'embarrassing moment' from the past with each other.

Laughter ball Throw an imaginary ball backwards and forwards between you, move further and further away from one another to make it more difficult to catch. Grunt when throwing, laugh when catching – now improvise!

Tummy laughs Lie down comfortably on your backs, one of you lying with your head on the other's tummy, then start to laugh gently…

Pretend conversations Imagine you are royalty, or TV presenters, or secret spies and improvise a 'serious' conversation in character.

Laugh in the face of fear Take it in turns to pick something you are worried or anxious about and declare one out loud, for example, 'I feel scared every time I drive on the motorway… I laugh in the face of this thought, HA, HA, ha, ha, ha, ha' (your friend should laugh along with you).

Gibberish story Pick an ordinary event from today to recount in your own made-up language using nonsense sounds, words and accompanying gestures; embellish your story for artistic effect. Your partner must pretend to understand every word and can ask you questions.

Back-to-back laugh Sit back-to-back somewhere comfortable so you can feel your partner's back against yours. Start to laugh gently…

Sumo laughter Imagine you are both Sumo wrestlers and challenge each other with slow-motion stances and heavy grunts. Try and wrestle one another onto the sofa or some other soft landing – no health and safety with this one!

Laughter exercises are incredibly contagious in group settings. In the next chapter we will learn about Laughter Yoga – a method that can help small and large groups of people to laugh together, play together and enjoy the full benefits of healthy laughter on a regular basis.

'Joy is the
feeling of
grinning on
the inside.'

MELBA COLGROVE

laughter yoga

Laughter Yoga encourages people to meet together on a regular basis to laugh freely for health, peace and happiness. Ever since it started in India over 20 years ago, Laughter Yoga has helped to improve the wellbeing of individuals and communities world-wide. Thanks to its existence, laughter clubs in every corner of the globe are emerging; a testament to the positive impact, durability and evolving nature of the Laughter Yoga movement.

THE ORIGINS OF LAUGHTER YOGA

Laughter Yoga is a method of voluntary laughter that brings people together from all walks of life for health and happiness. It was devised in 1995, by Dr Madan Kataria and his wife Madhuri.

THE ULTIMATE AIM OF LAUGHTER YOGA IS WORLD PEACE THROUGH LAUGHTER.

Dr Kataria was working as a physician in Mumbai in India and he was convinced of the many health benefits of laughter. Madan wanted to find a simple way for people to laugh frequently and unconditionally without the need for jokes or comedy. Together with Madhuri, he invented a way of combining laughter exercises with breathing techniques and committed himself to encouraging others to laugh on a regular basis. Laughter Yoga is a combination of deep yogic breathing, playfulness and laughter exercises and is now practised in over 75 countries.

The principles of Laughter Yoga are simple and effective: choose to bring laughter to the body as a form of exercise and with willingness and playfulness and it will soon turn to real laughter. Laughter Yoga is currently practised in a range of different organisations and places worldwide, including hospices, hospitals, schools, universities, prisons, refugee camps as well as large corporations and businesses.

'If you laugh you change; and when you change – the whole world changes.'

DR. MADAN KATARIA

Laughter club leaders are all trained according to the Laughter Yoga standards set out by Dr Kataria and people can undertake training to become a certified Laughter Yoga Leader, Laughter Yoga Teacher or Master Laughter Yoga Teacher.

LAUGHTER CLUBS

Laughter Yoga clubs have sprung up all around the world to encourage people of all ages to join together to laugh on a regular basis. The laughter clubs foster friendly connection with others, a sense of belonging, fun, exercise and wellbeing. Laughter clubs unite people and create laughter communities where laughter can be practised, explored and enjoyed by many in a safe and nourishing group environment. The Laughter Yoga exercises are easily adapted to the differing needs and physical capabilities of the participants and are therefore inclusive in their nature.

BUILDING THE LAUGHTER COMMUNITY

Every laughter club is different; some charge a small amount of money to cover costs and some are free of charge. Some of the laughter club leaders encourage their members to lead laughter exercises, become involved in the club organisation and to share games, creative ideas and playfulness with each other. Some meet in public spaces, such as parks and gardens, others in private houses or communal buildings – depending on the climate of each country. World Laughter Day is celebrated on the first Sunday in May all across the world.

THE LAUGHTER YOGA STRUCTURE

All Laughter Yoga sessions begin with an introduction to laughter and its many benefits, followed by a simple warm-up adapted for the club members. Deep breathing, smiling and simple, fun games that involve eye contact are utilised to enable people to relax and connect with each other at the beginning.

LAUGHTER YOGA EXERCISES

In between demonstrating laughter exercises, everyone takes two slow, deep breaths in and out to settle the body and rest. Clapping hands together in unison and chanting 'Ho, ho, ha, ha, ha' several times in rhythm between the exercises keeps everyone together, creates group rapport and lends structure to the sessions. The clapping re-energises participants and the chanting uses the laughter sounds, bringing in fresh oxygen to the body in short, easy steps. Everything is adapted to the needs of the group: clapping and chanting can be slowed according to the physical abilities of the people present if necessary and the exercises can be done seated, standing or lying down.

SIX LAUGHTER YOGA EXERCISES FOR GROUPS

During these group laughter exercises you are encouraged to join in as enthusiastically as you can, to allow yourself to pretend, imagine and be silly together for the sheer fun of it.

PARTICIPANTS ARE ENCOURAGED NOT TO TALK, AS TALKING ACTIVATES THE MORE RECENT, COGNITIVE PART OF THE BRAIN ASSOCIATED WITH LANGUAGE.

The Laughter Yoga process encourages this part of the brain to take a rest for a while to allow the more primitive side of the brain associated with laughter to awaken.

1. GREETING LAUGHTER

Take it in turns to greet everyone in the group warmly with eye contact and laughter instead of a verbal greeting as you shake their hands; bow to them, high-five them or use another playful type of greeting. Any type of laughter is to be encouraged, making the greetings as enthusiastic as possible. Make that person feel as valued and appreciated as possible, even if you have only just met them.

2. MILKSHAKE LAUGHTER

(This exercise can be adapted to suit any type of beverage.) Hold out two imaginary glasses in front of you, one in each hand. Cheekily pour the contents of one glass into the other with a playful 'Whooo' noise, and then pour some back into the other glass with an 'Aaaaah' noise. When you have done that, shake up the drink in both hands with a gentle laugh, hold eye contact with someone in the group, take a deep breath in and tip the drink into your mouth with a hearty laugh. Repeat with smaller or larger glasses as required. Throw the drink over someone – be creative.

3. LAUGHTER STEW

Stand with a partner by a large, imaginary cooking pot; together, start to make an imaginary stew by throwing in cupfuls of laughs, ladlefuls of guffaws, sprinkles of giggles and lashings of cackles. Stir with large spoons saying 'Mmmmm'. Lift up the spoons, slurp up the mixture noisily to taste it, and then pretend to spit out the stew with laughter. Add your own creative ingredients…

4. DRIVING LAUGHTER

Pretend to start up a decrepit old car engine by turning the ignition and laughing at the same time. However the laugh fades away when the engine doesn't fire up properly. Maintain eye contact with the other members of the group as you try to start the engine three times and the laughter fades away on each occasion. However on the fourth go, you turn the ignition, press down on the accelerator, grab the wheel, and let your laughter instantly propel your car all around the room – watch out for other drivers!

5. LAUGHTER ORCHESTRA

The conductor stands and tests out all the laughs in the group with a conducting baton; low, medium, high-pitched laughter, then quiet, medium and loud laughs with different gestures. After several rehearsals, they conduct a piece of creative laughter music from the group, which can descend from choreographed laughs into glorious free laughter chaos…

6. LAUGHING AT OURSELVES

This is a heart-warming exercise as everyone walks around the room, pointing at themselves and laughing at the same time. We realise it is okay to laugh at ourselves in an understanding and affectionate way. This exercise really helps encourages us to lighten up, and not to take ourselves, or life too seriously.

LAUGHTER MEDITATION
OR FREE LAUGHTER

After several laughter yoga exercises – there are literally
thousands – you can sit in a circle or lie down on the
floor on your back in a circle very close to one another.
Have your eyes closed or open, depending on what
is comfortable for your group. In your own time, start
to smile and chuckle gently, inviting your own natural
laughter to emerge. Rest and relax whenever you want
to throughout the process and laugh as much as you
like. Laughing freely with others is a liberating and
releasing experience. Allow your laughter space and
time, do not rush or force it and don't compare yourself
to others. Remember, your laughter is unique and some
days you may laugh heartily and other days you may
simply want to smile and listen. Accept it all lovingly.

'We don't laugh because we're happy – we're happy because we laugh.'

WILLIAM JAMES

LAUGHTER RELAXATION

'Tension is who we think we ought to be; relaxation is who we are.' Chinese Proverb

Laughter relaxes and re-balances us. It releases our mind, our muscles and our grip on life. When we laugh we can shake off the tension, worries and frustrations that weigh us down. Laughing reduces the size of our fears and renews us to the core. It stabilises situations and creates distance between us and our problems. It brings clarity, fresh perspective and renewed energy to old habits.

LAUGHTER EASES SITUATIONS, BRINGING LIGHTNESS, CALM AND A PERVADING SENSE OF PEACE. IT RETURNS US HOME.

After laughing heartily we flow into an experience of peace and relaxation that is sublime. We often sigh deeply, releasing any remainders of tension as our bodies enjoy the deep sensations of relaxation, tranquillity and serenity. It is important to notice and savour these feelings; allowing the body to settle after its aerobic laughter workout and to return to stillness.

We cannot be laughing all the time; to enjoy the full effects of laughter we also need to rest, to be quiet, to lie undisturbed and to access silence. Taking time to be still after laughing brings a sense of interconnectedness, deep wordless peace and a sense of oneness.

RELAXATION: SEATED OR LYING DOWN

To enhance relaxation after laughing you may want to use:

Mindful body scans or mindful breathing

Quiet music or gentle sounds

Guided relaxations

Silence

Mantras, affirmations

Gentle, slow stretching and breathing

Gentle
smiling

The nature
around you
(if outdoors)

Candles, scents,
aromatherapy oils
or incense sticks

Visualisation,
pictures or
memories

For more details of Laughter
Yoga around the world see
www.laughteryoga.org

Touch
or gentle
massage

everyday laughter

The more we
laugh, the more
we laugh. Building
laughter opportunities
into everyday life increases
our chances of laughing heartily,
spontaneously and unexpectedly.
Each day there are new discoveries to be
made as the laughter journey is a continuous
and varied one. We never stop learning about
our laughter and benefit from it most when it is
valued, shared and occurs frequently. One way
to ensure this is to develop a laughter practice
that suits our individual circumstances.

DEVELOPING A LAUGHTER PRACTICE

Why do we need to practise laughing?

In our normal, everyday life there may be only a few precious moments of the day that make us laugh or smile. Sometimes we can go for long periods of time without a smile or even a subtle snigger.

We may be living on our own, or with people we don't normally laugh with, or we may be going through a difficult time and may not have laughed for ages. Even if we already laugh regularly there is always more to discover about ourselves and our laughter. And it's nourishing for us (see chapter one if you need any reminders).

When we focus on something it becomes more prominent. Practising laughter daily helps our laughter to become natural and easy and close to the surface of our lives – more accessible. Laughter becomes a well-known friend and ally, in joyful and troublesome times alike.

We will never be bored if we can turn on our laughter tap. Laughter is like a muscle; the more we use it, the stronger it gets. Practising laughter helps to transform it from a conscious, voluntary exercise to natural, involuntary, spontaneous laughter that bubbles up from within.

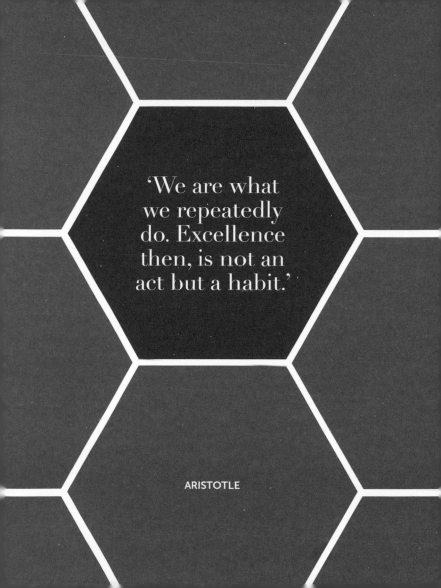

'We are what we repeatedly do. Excellence then, is not an act but a habit.'

ARISTOTLE

TIPS FOR A DAILY LAUGH

For laughter to become part of your daily life there are a number of things you need to bear in mind to help open yourself up to every opportunity.

BE CLEAR ON YOUR WHY

Your why will be unique to you and your life. *Why is it important to you to laugh every day? What will it give you?* Write down everything you will gain from laughing every day. *What would happen if you didn't do this?* Draw a symbol to symbolise your laughter and what it gives you. Pin it above your desk or in your kitchen where you see it every day. Move it around if you stop noticing it.

DECIDE YOUR HOW

How are you going to laugh, for how long, with anyone else or on your own? At what time will you start laughing every day and for how long? How many days will you commit to doing the practice for to begin with (45 days is a great place to start)? How will you record this (make it easy, maybe just a tick in your diary)? Design a manageable, achievable plan and start gently, maybe simply smiling each day if that is suitable, graduating to gentle chuckles.

Will you need a regular quiet space or time each day?
How will you engineer that? What could get in the way
of this happening?

VISUALISE WHAT IT IS YOU WOULD LIKE TO HAVE HAPPEN

Before running a race, athletes mentally rehearse each step of the run in close detail. They see themselves running; they feel in their mind how it will be to be running freely, effortlessly, easily. They visualise each step of the run from doing up their laces to crossing the finishing line. Using the same technique with your laughter practice will guide your mind to success even before you start to chuckle. Imagine yourself laughing every day in glorious, colourful images and FEEL what it will be like in advance. Even anticipating laughter releases endorphins!

BUILD IN DAILY REWARDS AND ENCOURAGEMENT

We all learn better when we feel relaxed and supported.

How encouraging are you being of yourself every day? What are you going to say to yourself during and after each practice? How loving and supportive will you be in making this change?

Do not only celebrate the end of your 45 days of practice, celebrate each session, each smile and deep breath, each chuckle and laugh. Notice how your body feels before, during and after the exercises or practice. Calibrate what feels good, what feels right for you. Change the practice as necessary. It's *your* practice.

BUILD IN FAILURE

None of us are infallible and unless we prepare for setbacks and mistakes then we are aiming for perfection and that is too high for the bar to be set. Allow yourself one or two setbacks in the system to begin with. Visualise how you will support yourself through these times and how you will get back on track the next day. Look closely and honestly at what caused the setback and ask yourself if your 'why' is still as relevant as it was or whether it needs tweaking. Re-connect with your 'why' and plan in another step to avoid falling in the same hole again. *How can this be avoided next time?* Then let go of the setback, smile and imagine your resolve becoming stronger and stronger as you restart your daily practice.

BE ACCOUNTABLE TO SOMEONE

Gather support. The most successful changes we make are when we feel the need to do something and there is also something urging us NOT to stop. It may be that we have made a promise to someone, or they are depending on us, or we feel we will let ourselves down if we do not do the daily practice. It could be that we have gone public with our intentions and do not want to go back on that commitment.

MAKE IT FUN!

If your practice is enjoyable it will be easy to repeat. Laughing is great fun so keep it light-hearted and joyful by not forcing it, or by imposing restrictions and 'shoulds' into the practice. Start gently and learn to adore your laughter. Be playful with it and don't take it too seriously! It can become a daily reminder to choose a lighter way, to let go of solemnity and to access the power within which is limitless. Your laugh does not need to rely on external conditions; it can emerge given encouragement, surrender and practice.

'If at first you don't succeed … so much for skydiving.'

HENNY YOUNGMAN

LAUGHTER INTEGRATION

Here are some ways to incorporate laughter practise into everyday life.

Laugh in the shower.

Laugh when you drive up to a red traffic light.

Laugh when you flush the toilet.

Laugh when you get home.

Skip more.

Wear your pants on your head.

When you are frustrated find a quiet place to shout and scream and revel in it until it turns to laughter.

Share a joke of the day with someone, every day.

Create your own daily laugh.

Laugh as you do the housework (particularly useful when cleaning toilets).

Do a silly dance.

Ask unusual questions of people.

Look for the funny in ordinary moments.

Have a pillow fight.

Laugh on the way to work or the shops, walk and laugh or drive and laugh (possibly more dangerous).

Spend time with people who are good fun.

Imagine your trip to work is your playground.

Be spontaneous.

Hide from your friends or family and then jump out on them.

Be ultra, ultra-serious.

Speak in a strange voice.

Sing heartily, making up your own lyrics.

Keep a list of anything that makes you laugh or smile and keep adding to it.

Do something silly or frivolous.

Mimic yourself in a bad mood.

Answer the telephone with a laugh.

Whistle, yodel and make strange and wonderful noises with your mouth.

See how many different places in your house or local area you can laugh.

Dare to take a risk every day.

Wear brightly coloured or outrageous clothes.

Take silly selfies or photos.

Share conversations with strangers and ask them what makes them laugh.

Tell a funny story to anyone who will listen, laugh as you tell it, even if they don't find it funny they will enjoy hearing you laughing.

LETTING GO: THE SECRET INGREDIENT

It seems that just when we think we know where we are going or what the future might hold everything changes and our plans go awry. Change is the ever-present constant so we can either fight to control it or accept it when it happens.

Remember times when things you had planned carefully for didn't happen... what was the result?

Sometimes it worked out for the better – sometimes not – but we have to face the fact sooner or later that we cannot control everything. This may be difficult for the perfectionists amongst us but it may come as a bit of relief too. Times like this are when laughter comes into its own. It reminds us that we are deliciously human, flawed and susceptible to blunders, mishaps and horrendously embarrassing (and very funny) moments.

It may not be easy immediately: for example, if you have walked into your boss's office while singing loudly, to find a team of senior managers in the middle of a serious meeting, you may not be able to laugh straight away. You may need time to withdraw, apologise, give yourself some space – and then find the humour in the event afterwards.

THE SOONER WE CAN START TO PLAY WITH OUR PAIN OR OUR MISTAKES THE SOONER WE CAN LET GO, FORGIVE OURSELVES AND MOVE ON.

TIPS FOR LETTING GO
AND LAUGHING MORE

Think of a motto to encourage you to lighten up: 'it'll all come out in the wash' or 'life is ridiculous' or even 'that went swimmingly'.

Replay the event in your mind to 'can-can' music or something equally silly.

Devise 'it could have been worse…' scenarios in your head so you can start playing with ideas.

Imagine how your favourite comedian would deal with a similar situation.

Imagine yourself telling the story and laughing out loud.

Imagine what your three-year-old niece would do.

Play, hum or sing the song 'Let it Go' from the movie Frozen, complete with over-the-top gestures.

Keep breathing.
Deep, deep breathing...

Find someone who will find the event funnier than you, and tell them the story.

Accept it's just not funny and declare this to the world repeatedly with fervour 'It's just NOT funny'.

Think, 'This will be funny in 3 / 13 / 30 years' time.'

Cry, gnash your teeth, stomp and wail to your heart's delight until the urge to smile becomes too much.

LAUGHTER EVOLUTION

Our laughter exists on a constantly shifting scale, and our position on the laughter continuum at any one moment depends on our attitude, awareness and openness. There are no laughter experts. Some people have become so at ease with themselves that they love laughing, laugh freely and spontaneously and happily share their laughter with others. These people are great to be with and to model, as their laughter is highly contagious. Some of them have been introduced to laughter from an early age and others have learned along the way.

ANYONE CAN BECOME A 'FREE' LAUGHER GIVEN TIME, PATIENCE AND ENCOURAGEMENT.

THE LAUGHTER CONTINUUM

Beginning to laugh	Frequent practice	Laughing freely
Practising exercises	Finding exercises easier	Loving own laugh
Self-conscious	Deeper enjoyment	Deep connection
Intentional laughter	Ability to savour	Spontaneous laughter
Curious	Creative and experimental	Laughing with life
Controlled	Feeling lighter in oneself	Lightness and experiences of deep joy
Willing	Playing more	Playful and mischievous
Structured	Occasional loss of control	Surrender of control
Noticing laughs	Enjoying effects of laughter	Sense of inner peace and wellbeing
Laughing for self	Able to laugh at self	Laughing inexplicably
Developing self compassion	Encouraging to self	Deep love for others

FOLLOWING THE PATH TOWARDS LAUGHTER

We are all constantly learning, exploring and evolving and we can be anywhere along the continuum at any one time. The ever-present strand that is woven throughout is self-love and kindness. We all need to keep a 'beginner's mind' where laughter is concerned, to let go of any attachment to being a 'free laugher' or a 'good laugher'. It is too easy to become tangled in the messy human web of life and we constantly need to pick ourselves up, brush ourselves down, laugh and step back on the path.

We are all in this journey together; we are all imperfectly perfect.

LAUGHTER UNITES US ALL; IT LIGHTS US UP FROM WITHIN AND REMINDS US WHO WE ARE.

'A good time
to laugh is any
time you can.'

MELBA COLGROVE

the gift of laughter

Life can easily become ever so serious if we let it. We can become so bogged down with the everyday burdens of day-to-day living; responsibilities, worries and troubles, that our mind and body become clogged with anxiety and stress. This can happen overnight or slowly and insidiously over a long period of time. We can forget or refuse to play, to connect, to ask for help, to give love to ourselves or to others. We can forget what fun feels like. We stop laughing. We may withdraw from life, from joy and from others.

It is crucial to understand that our laughter never leaves us; we just lose touch with it. Once we start to let go of our tight grip on life and reach out to others, replenish our energies and begin the vital journey of loving ourselves deeply and unconditionally, it gently starts to re-emerge. Laughter is an expression of the soul and merely waits in the wings for you to remember that you are wonderful, just as you are.

ONE LAUGH

Laughter is magical. It transports us from the confines of our minds into another realm altogether; an expansive space where there is more light, more peace and more love.

Laughter is irresistible to the heart. It calls the spirit within to rise up and dance in union. We are all drawn to the mystical sound of laughter, to its healing powers and to its life affirming qualities.

Laughing freely is loving freely: loving ourselves, loving life, loving this imperfect and troublesome world that we inhabit here on Earth.

Laughter leads us back to the region of the heart, where love flows easily and freely, restoring balance and harmony to body and mind.

Laughing heartily with others connects us at our core and reminds us that we are all the same. We all experience deep sorrows and profound joys in life and we need each other's support in order to thrive. With laughter comes greater understanding and true forgiveness.

LAUGHTER OPENS US TO OUR ESSENTIAL ETERNAL ESSENCE, WHICH IS LOVE.

Embracing the laughter path leads to yet more joy, more possibilities, more expansion of awareness and the understanding that we are here on Earth to join with others, to help others and to celebrate together.

Our troubled world needs more love, light and laughter than ever before. Together we can bring more peace, understanding and acceptance into the world through continually reaching out to others, one laugh at a time.

YET TO CHANGE THE WORLD WE HAVE TO BEGIN WITH OURSELVES.

Can you imagine a world where terrorists loosen their grip on their anger, where frightened enemies slowly turn away from war and destruction and begin to listen to the peace and joy that resides within? Laughter gives us a glimpse of this vision.

Finding ways to access the peace within us can begin with simply smiling. As we dive deeper and deeper into the well of laughter we may discover even more than we ever thought possible.

'The human race
has only one
really effective
weapon and that
is laughter.'

MARK TWAIN

'The sound of laughter is like the vaulted dome of a temple of happiness.'

MILAN KUNDERA

LAUGHTER BLESSING

Wherever you may travel, may your laughter journey be fun, surprising and honest.

May you stay open to laughter even in the direst of circumstances and even in the darkest of places.

May you find laughter companions to share your journey and may you carry the eternal flame of laughter lightly in your heart.

May you find your own ways to laugh, to dance and to make merry, and then ways to relax and surrender to the peace that passes all understanding.

May you continue to light up the world in your own, unique way and shine like the limitless, loving soul that you are.

SAFETY NOTES

Laughter is a healthy and natural complementary form of exercise for the mind, body and spirit. However, as it involves some physical strain and an increase in intra-abdominal pressure, it does not suit everyone. Like all forms of exercise, people with medical conditions should first take advice from their doctor. Laughter healing is NOT recommended for people with:

- Advanced (bleeding) piles
- Any kind of hernia
- Any persistent cough
- Any condition with acute symptoms
- Epilepsy
- Heart disease
- High blood pressure
- Incontinence of urine
- Major psychiatric disorders
- Severe back pain
- A recent history of surgery (within three months)
- In the first trimester of pregnancy

If you have any of the conditions listed, are recovering from any surgery or have any medical conditions or concerns, it is essential that you consult a trained medical professional for guidance before practising any of the exercises contained within this book.

ALSO Please don't laugh and eat at the same time, and swimming and laughing doesn't work either, I've tried it and you just end up sinking.

QUOTES WERE TAKEN FROM

Albert Einstein was a theoretical physicist. He is renowned for developing the general theory of relativity and received the Nobel Prize for Physics in 1921.

Aristotle was one of the greatest philosophers from ancient Greece. His work has had a long-lasting influence on the development of all Western philosophical theories.

Arnold H. Glasow was an American publisher, journalist and humorist, who contributed a column regularly to *Reader's Digest*.

Bob Hope was an American comedian and actor, who appeared in over 70 films during his show-business career.

Dr. Seuss (Theodor Seuss Geisel) was an American author and illustrator who is best known for his children's books, including *The Cat in the Hat* and *Green Eggs and Ham*.

Lord Byron (George Gordon Byron) was a British poet and leading figure in the Romantic movement. Notoriously flamboyant, Byron was celebrated as much for his excessive lifestyle as his writing.

Henry 'Henny' Youngman was an American comedian and violinist who was famous for his simple one-liner jokes told in rapid-fire succession.

Mark Twain (Samuel Langhorne Clemens) was an American author who wrote *The Adventures of Huckleberry Finn*, which is often called the great American novel.

Melba Colgrove is the author of books such as *How to Survive the Loss of a Love*.

Milan Kundera is a Czech-born writer now living in France, whose works include *The Unbearable Lightness of Being*.

Mother Theresa was a Roman Catholic nun and missionary, who was canonized after her death.

Dr. Madan Kataria is an Indian physician who popularized laughter yoga, which he wrote about in *Laugh for No Reason*.

Shirley MacLaine is an American actor, author and activist who won an Academy Award for her role in *Terms of Endearment*.

William James was an American philosopher and psychologist, considered one of the leading thinkers of the nineteenth century.

William Shakespeare was an English playwright, poet and actor. Considered one of the greatest writers in the English language, his works include *Hamlet*, *Macbeth* and *King Lear*.

Thank you Ed, Isaac and Ollie for your endless support, encouragement and playfulness.
I love you to bits.

Grateful thanks to Madan and Madhuri Kataria, the Chichester Laughter Club and the global family of laughers, leaders and teachers around the world.

Love, peace and laughter blessings to you all.

Publishing Director Sarah Lavelle
Commissioning Editor Lisa Pendreigh
Copy Editor Katie Hewett
Creative Director Helen Lewis
Designer and Illustrator Emily Lapworth
Production Controller Emily Noto
Production Director Vincent Smith

First published in 2017 by
Quadrille Publishing
Pentagon House
52–54 Southwark Street
London SE1 1UN
www.quadrille.co.uk
www.quadrille.com

Quadrille is an imprint of
Hardie Grant
www.hardiegrant.com.au

Reprinted in 2017
10 9 8 7 6 5 4 3 2

Text © 2017 Lisa Sturge
Artwork, design and layout
© 2017 Quadrille Publishing Ltd

Cataloguing in Publication Data:
a catalogue record for this book is available from the British Library.

ISBN: 978 184949 956 9

Printed in China